AF477568

# wallpaper

**Published by the Historic Houses Trust of New South Wales**

The Mint, 10 Macquarie Street,
Sydney NSW 2000 Australia
T 02 8239 2288  www.hht.net.au

ISBN 978-1-876991-37-1

© 2010 Historic Houses Trust
of New South Wales



Head of Publications, Susan Sedgwick
Edited by Sarah Fitzherbert
Designed by Emma Warfield
Picture rights and permissions
by Alice Livingstone
Pre-press by Spitting Image, Sydney
Printed by Print Plus, China

National Library of Australia
Cataloguing-in-Publication entry
Author: Lech, Michael, 1965-
Title: Wallpaper / Michael Lech.
ISBN: 9781876991371 (hbk.)

Notes: Bibliography.
Subjects: Wallpaper—Australia—History.
Wallpaper—History.
Other Authors/Contributors: Historic
Houses Trust of New South Wales.
Dewey Number: 747.3

**Cover: 'The Aylsham'**, designed by C F A Voysey for Essex & Co, England, 1893

**Back cover quote:** *Artistic homes; or, how to furnish with taste: a handbook for all housekeepers,* Ward, Lock & Co, London, 1880, p21.

**Endpapers: 'Maidenhair'** [monotone], designed by Cherie Miles for David Miles Handprinted Wallpaper, Sydney, c1973

**Pages 104–5:** Stained glass pattern (detail) © Estate of Florence Broadhurst

# wallpaper

Michael Lech

# preface

*Wallpaper* is the first book in our Historic Houses Trust Collection series. Each title will bring to life a slice of the diverse Historic Houses Trust (HHT) collections. Unique in Australia, the HHT manages 12 very different properties – historic houses, public buildings and museums – and over 400,000 items. The Collection series will celebrate particular features of these extensive collections and interest those passionate about houses and gardens, design and the decorative arts.

This book showcases the wallpaper collection of the HHT's Caroline Simpson Library & Research Collection, the leading library in Australia dedicated to the history of house and garden design and interior furnishing. Housed at our head office at The Mint in Sydney, the library has for the past two decades been actively acquiring wallpapers ranging from small fragments to complete rolls and sample books dating from about 1840 to the present day.

While many of the designs reproduced in this book are visually appealing, our primary reason for acquiring a new wallpaper for the collection is not *good* design but rather the wallpaper's association with, or provenance to, an Australian home, merchant or manufacturer. By choosing wallpapers on the basis of provenance rather than design or taste, which vary over time, we intend the wallpapers in the collection to offer a glimpse into the domestic lives of Australians since 1840.

# wallpaper in australia

Australians have had a long love affair with wallpaper. But, as in all affairs, there have been times of great affection and others of disenchantment and derision. Climate, changes in fashion, concerns about cleanliness in the home and developments in paint and wallpaper technology have influenced the relationship. However, for more than 200 years Australians of all income levels and from all parts of the country have taken advantage of the colour, pattern and texture afforded by wallpaper.

The use of wallpaper was at its peak in Australia between the mid-19th century and the beginning of World War I. The mechanisation of the industry in England in 1839, together with the gradual removal of English excise tax up to 1861, meant that huge numbers of inexpensive designs became available. An English architect, C Bruce Allen, wrote in 1857 that 'the commoner sorts of paper now being so cheap … the walls of every cottage living-room, at least, should be covered with it, as conducing so much to the cheerfulness and comfort of the inmates'.[1] (The *Australian builders price book* for 1862 lists the cheapest wallpapers, 'common pulps on self coloured paper', as priced from fourpence to ninepence per roll.) When the eighth edition of Allen's book was printed in 1900, his comment about the cheapness of wallpaper was unaltered. Indeed, over this time the prices of wallpaper had barely changed. In 1914 Sydney department store Anthony Hordern & Sons' general catalogue lists 'dark pulps' from threepence halfpenny and 'light pulps' from fourpence per roll.

'Pulps' were just one of a variety of different types of wallpaper. They were the cheapest available because a pattern was printed directly onto the surface of the wallpaper without any preparatory background colour being applied, the colour of the paper itself becoming a significant part of the design. Other categories of wallpaper found up until the early 20th century included 'grounds', which had a background colour applied before the pattern was added, 'satins' or 'silks', 'micas', 'flocks' and 'golds'. Each had a different surface treatment and was priced accordingly.

Wallpaper was not only readily available to all Australians, it was used throughout the country both in cities and rural areas, though statistics suggest that it featured less in the warmer northern regions. Nevertheless, wallpaper was installed in 1863 at a relatively hot and remote homestead in Exmoor, central Queensland, by Rachel Henning, her sister, brother and a station hand.[2] In timber slab huts throughout the Australian countryside, wallpaper not only provided colour and pattern but, by covering the gaps in the slabs, also offered extra insulation. The walls of most such dwellings, however, were first lined with other material such as canvas to stop the paper splitting at the joins. Architect Fred Harrison stated in 1889 that 'it is common custom (particularly in the bush), to line walls, partitions, and ceilings, with "canvas and paper"' and that 'coarse, cheap, hessian, with a strong fibre is better than finer cloth'.[3] There are numerous examples in the Caroline Simpson Library & Research Collection of the use of hessian and other cloth lining as backing for wallpaper throughout the 19th century, from wealthy residences like Aberglasslyn near Maitland and New South Wales Parliament House to a humble slab hut near Conargo in the south-west of the state.

The task of wallpapering often fell to the women of the household, especially when professional paperhangers were unavailable or considered too pricey. Many historians accept that after the 1860s it was women's job to choose and look after household furnishings, especially in middle-class homes.[4] An image from an 1872 article in the *Town & Country Journal*, entitled 'How to paper a room'[5], shows two women engaged in papering the room of a country house, and architect Fred Harrison claimed in 1889 that 'ladies in the bush often do a little amateur paper hanging'.[6] Although professional paperhangers were almost exclusively men, illustrations in newspapers and magazines throughout most of the 20th century more often depicted women installing wallpaper in the home.

Coal fires and fly spots were common causes of damage to wallpaper but its low cost meant that replacement was easy and frequent. In addition, one or several layers of wallpaper could provide an excellent cover for uneven or cracked walls. Multiple layers of 19th- and early-20th-century wallpaper have been found on the walls of even the humblest of Australian homes. In a modest worker's cottage in the inner Sydney suburb of Pyrmont, 11 layers of wallpaper dating from the early 1840s to the 1880s were uncovered in one room, probably used as a parlour. And the use of multiple layers of wallpaper continued beyond the 19th century. According to a Melbourne decorator in 1908, 'in the painting and repapering of the ordinary residence in and about the suburbs of Melbourne it is the usual custom … for the paperhanger to paste one paper on top of the old one without first removing the old paper'.[7] This practice continued well beyond 1908; in one room of a timber slab hut in Prospect, west of Sydney, 26 layers of wallpaper plus some newspaper lining, all installed between 1908 and the 1950s, were uncovered.

Although the hanging of a new wallpaper over the top of previous layers appears to have been common practice, by the end of the 19th century it was also the subject of criticism. According to the *Town & Country Journal* in 1902, laws had existed in the United States of America for many years compelling decorators to remove old layers of wallpaper before hanging new ones. In Australia, where no such law existed, old wallpapers were, according to some critics, literally poisoning residents: 'the greatest danger comes from a gas, deleterious to the health, which is generated from old and decayed paste and size, dirt and smoke' in the hidden layers of wallpaper.[8] Architects Terry & Oakden had claimed some years before that the 'pores' of wallpaper would in time 'get clogged with impurities' but also that the 'more brilliant coloured papers are apt to contain metallic poisons, which are thrown off, and injuriously affect the occupants of the room'.[9] Wallpaper pigments contained a host of potentially poisonous substances but the most notorious wallpapers were the green ones, which often contained an arsenic component.

Arsenic green (copper arsenite), also known as 'Scheele's green', was used in some fabrics, paint and wallpaper throughout the 19th century. The danger of arsenic in wallpaper was first suspected in Germany in the 1830s but little was done to restrict its use in wallpaper in England and Australia. In 1858 a select committee of the English House of Lords heard that the largest quantity of arsenic used

in England was employed in the manufacturing of wallpaper.[10] Five years later Rachel Henning wrote to her sister that she was happy to live with her pretty, newly installed wallpaper in Australia that was a 'true arsenic green' because 'in this airy abode I do not think we are likely to be poisoned'.[11] The exact chemical reaction that produced the dangerous gaseous substance remained unknown, however, until late in the 19th century when it was discovered to be caused by the combination of arsenic with damp and fungi living on wallpaper paste. Arsenic was not completely removed from all wallpaper until the early 20th century.

Pests were another problem, particularly in warmer climates where for many insects wallpaper was the preferred plat du jour. According to the *Brisbane Courier* in 1878, wallpaper afforded 'great facilities for the study of entomology, but [was] otherwise objectionable' and paint should be used in preference.[12] By 1890 'Beryl' from the *Illustrated Sydney News* emphasised that 'wall-papers in this climate [Australia] are unsuitable and objectionable' chiefly because 'they harbour and feed silverfish, who increase and multiply and fatten on the paste used to fix the papers to the wall'.[13] In 1914 the trade journal the *Australasian*

*Decorator and Painter* described silverfish as 'an ever increasing pest' often attacking wallpapers in the home, though the recommended treatment with hydrocyanic acid gas cannot have been a very healthy solution for residents. In 1920 A V Sugden, chairman of Wall Paper Manufacturers Ltd of England, the largest wallpaper company in the world, wrote to the same journal offering a more people-friendly solution after assigning his own laboratory staff to investigate the problem.[14] The size of the Australian market meant that in 1938 the same company donated money to a researcher at the University of Melbourne who developed an anti–silverfish solution that could be sprayed onto wallpapers.[15]

Silverfish may have been an ongoing nuisance but in the late 19th century it was concern for cleanliness in the home that occupied the time of many middle-class home owners. The mass of ornament and drapery typically found in late-Victorian interiors was criticised for harbouring dust and grime, and wallpaper was one of the most undesirable elements according to critics in newspapers, women's journals and architectural trade papers. Despite the bad press, Australians continued to hang wallpaper and now also had the choice of newly invented wipeable or washable products. As early as 1852 Sydney merchant Henry Woolley advertised the sale of 'a marble paper, particularly well adapted for a hot climate, as it will bear washing by any servant'.[16] In the early 1870s the introduction of new 'sanitary' papers, printed using oil colours rather than distemper, allowed home owners to wipe dirt and dust from the wallpaper without fear that the colours would run. They could also apply varnish to sanitary papers to provide an extra layer of protection. This was especially recommended in high-use areas and for the dado, the lower section of a wall below the chair rail, which was more prone to being soiled. This treatment, however, usually darkened the colours of the wallpaper.

Embossed wallcoverings were another development of the last quarter of the 19th century. These were championed even by critics of wallpaper, principally because of their hygienic qualities. As well as being available in pleasing designs, they were impervious to dust, usually easy to clean, durable and even able to be painted over. The first to appear were brands like Tynecastle and Lincrusta-Walton in the 1870s. These were soon followed by a raft of imitators like Anaglypta, Lignomur and Cordelova, all of which were similar wallcoverings made from a variety of materials including cork and rubber, rag and wood pulp.

From around the 1860s the gradual appearance of domestic advisers who wrote books and newspaper columns for a growing middle class signalled a greater focus on decoration in the home. An article in the *Sydney Mail* in 1878, reprinted from the English journal *Queen*, declared 'house decoration is quite the rage'.[17] Domestic advisers were typically prescriptive in the types of furnishings, colours and patterns they recommended. One concern was that certain wallpaper patterns might appear 'wearisome' after only a short interval, or that formal, rigid designs like diamonds, stars or stripes might set 'nervous, fidgety people at work to count them'.[18] Selecting a wallpaper design for a bedroom was especially important because of the room's function as a place of convalescence. Consequently, it was important 'to avoid any outré forms, which the eye of a restless invalid, condemned to weary hours of solitude, could torture into the form or face of demon or grotesque horror'.[19] The wrong paper may even prove disastrous if it were to give 'a muddy mottled appearance not in the least attractive' to a person who otherwise has a 'healthy clear complexion'.[20]

Not only were certain wallpapers more appropriate for particular rooms, they should also be installed in a suitably 'artistic' manner. For example, after about 1870 the idea that one wallpaper could be used on all parts of the wall (and even the ceiling) in the one room was unthinkable to the taste-makers of the time. In his influential book *Hints on household taste in furniture, upholstery, and other details* (1868) Englishman Charles Eastlake recommended breaking up the wall surface into three: a dado, fill and frieze. Each was to be of a prescribed standard height and each was to have a certain preferred style — the fill, for example, should be in a lighter shade than the dado or frieze and with less pattern so that it would not compete with pictures hung over it. This fashion for tripartite wall division changed after about 1900 but commentators, wallpaper manufacturers and merchants, aided by diagrams or room views in journals, magazines, advertisements, brochures and other trade literature, continued to suggest the most up-to-date wall fashions throughout the 20th century.

Australian homes have typically followed the fashions in wall decoration common to Western countries around the world. Australians have also had little influence on the designs with which they have adorned their walls, as local wallpaper manufacturing remained the endeavour of a select few in this country at least until the 1970s. The vast majority of wallpapers used in Australian homes have been imported. Although some of the earliest recorded wallpaper imports were Chinese, and almost certainly handpainted papers, by the mid-19th century most local merchants were advertising the latest English and French designs. Several of the English, French and German exhibitors at the Melbourne International Exhibition of 1880–81 had local agents. However, the first reliable statistics for wallpaper imports, compiled in 1903 after the establishment of the Commonwealth of Australia, show that 82% of all wallpaper imports (in monetary terms) had come from England, the rest from Germany, the United States, Canada, Belgium and Japan.[21]

The English had pioneered the mechanisation of wallpaper production in 1839 and for the rest of that century manufacturing and exports grew at a rapid rate; eventually Britain became the world's pre-eminent wallpaper maker and supplier. Australians were quick to embrace the English product. In the 1850s and 60s Australia was the second largest market for British wallpaper after the USA, but from the 1870s onward it overtook the USA to claim the number one position. When in 1890 the English manufacturer Allan Cockshut & Co received from an Australian merchant the largest order in the company's history up to that time, Australia accounted for over 35% of all wallpaper exported from Britain, over £56,000 worth of stock.[22] Australia remained the largest consumer of British wallpaper until the 1920s.[23] During the first half of the 20th century, Britain consistently produced around three-quarters of all wallpaper imported into Australia. Preferential tariffs for British wallpapers also encouraged imports into Australia; in 1907 the general tariff on wallpapers was 20% compared to 15% for British-made, and by 1920 the general tariff had increased to 25%.[24]

Despite Australians being devotees of wallpaper, particularly from Britain, few ventured into the manufacturing side of the business. A combination of the large capital outlay required to establish commercial production and the fact that the Australian market was relatively small and isolated may have made it unviable to establish the economies of scale necessary to support manufacturing. Scant references have been found to 19th-century Australian wallpaper manufacturing. In 1851 Richard Guthridge of Melbourne boasted of his own 'paper manufactory', which was 'believed to be the only one in the southern hemisphere'.[25] At the Melbourne Intercolonial Exhibition of 1866–67 both C Carter and Jabez Clarke exhibited wallpaper designs, and at the Sydney International Exhibition of 1879–80 W Mote displayed 'wall-paper decorations'.[26] However, no physical evidence of Australian-made wallpaper from the 19th century is known to survive.

In the early years of the 20th century three Australian manufacturers started business: Gilkes & Co and Morrison's in Sydney and J W Williams in Adelaide. Local wallpaper manufacturing was encouraged by a change in wallpaper fashion. The use of wide or 'deep' friezes designed for the upper part of a wall became popular in the first decade of the 20th century and wallpaper panelling remained in style until the 1930s. This fashion allowed 'boutique' makers to operate and survive in a competitive environment. Gilkes & Co, Morrison's

and J W Williams all manufactured wallpapers by hand in small
workshops, using woodblocks and stencils, a practice popularised
by the likes of English wallpaper designer and entrepreneur Shand
Kydd. This required only a small capital outlay and no large
machinery or plant. However, these wallpapers were clearly aimed
at a wealthier market as they were more highly priced than imported,
mass-produced, machine-made papers.

The use of native flora or fauna as motifs was almost totally absent
from designs by the Australian commercial enterprises, although
it was common to student exercises at technical colleges in Sydney
and Melbourne and at craft exhibitions such as the First Australian
Exhibition of Women's Work 1907. It was eventually left to an English
firm, the Wall Paper Manufacturers Ltd, to produce a commercial
wallpaper that depicted Australian flora, firstly a frieze incorporating
waratah and flannel flowers in 1920, followed by others a year later
including one based on wattle blossom. In early 1920 the chairman
of the company, A V Sugden, had visited Australia and returned with
four books that assisted his designers in the replication of Australian
flora. One of those books was quite likely to have been RT Baker's
*The Australian flora in applied art: part 1, the waratah*, published in 1915, as
Sugden had asked Baker for his assessment of the waratah frieze,
to which Baker replied that he felt 'some little satisfaction that my
labours in Applied Art have now brought forth fruit'.[27] The decision
by Australian manufacturers not to depict local flora in their wallpaper
designs was a commercial one, which kept in mind the tastes of their
wealthy and possibly conservative clients. Conversely, Wall Paper

Manufacturers Ltd must have perceived some market potential in the use of Australian flora. It is unclear, however, whether or not its designs proved to be commercially successful and whether or not they were sold only into the Australian market.

The Australian wallpaper industry remained largely dormant from the 1930s to the late 1950s, perhaps partly because of a change in fashion. In 1928 when the stylish magazine *The Home* asked architects and other taste-makers their opinions on what to avoid in interior decoration, Sydney architect Gilbert Hughes expressed a commonly held view when he wrote, 'Avoid ornate wallpapers. Keep your walls plain, and if possible one tone for walls, woodwork and ceiling.'[28] By the 1930s much of fashionable society had rejected wallpaper in favour of plain or textured painted surfaces, forcing small Australian makers out of the market. The only known local wallcovering manufacturer in this period produced an embossed product called Fabrex, probably similar in composition to Anaglypta, but available only in single colours or two tones.[29]

The use of paint to decorate Australian walls had always been an option but until around the 1930s the most affordable paint, known as 'calsomine', was water-based and prone to flaking when exposed to damp conditions. After World War II, however, paint became a serious challenger to wallpaper as developments in paint technology allowed washable surfaces to become standard. There were also technological advances in wallpaper production, though fully washable vinyl-coated wallpapers invented soon after World War II were not commonly found in Australian homes until the 1960s. But wallpaper was clearly not used in Australia to the same extent as in the past. In the 1950s both New Zealand and the USA imported more British wallpapers than did Australia. And as late as 1965 the Australian wallpaper market was still being described as small because of our preference for painted surfaces; wallpaper consumption per capita in Australia was about a twelfth that of Britain and New Zealand.[30] That some of the latest designs were not available in Australia also hampered wallpaper use in this country. It was not until 1960 that a decade-long import quota restricting the importation of wallpapers to Australia was lifted, opening doors to new sources.[31] In 1963 an Australian distributor claimed that there were more wallpaper designs offered to Australians than to any other people in the world; designs were now imported from 18 different countries and approximately 2000 different patterns were offered.[32]

During the 1940s and 50s a number of Australian companies ventured into fabric printing but few made the leap to printing wallpapers. One exception was Falric in Melbourne, which printed woollen furnishing fabrics and matching wallpapers. By the late 1950s R Heiser of Sydney made the first Australian foray into the manufacture of machine-made wallpapers; the only known design was a single-coloured candy stripe available in a number of different colourways.[33] After this period a number of other Australian manufacturers emerged but they almost invariably used the screen-printing process that allowed small print runs for a select market. The earliest and best known was Florence Broadhurst whose company, called Australian Handprinted Wallpapers until 1969 and then Florence Broadhurst Wallpapers, employed a number of young local designers in its Sydney studios. By the early 1970s other Australian companies had entered the market, including David Miles Handprinted Wallpaper and Noel Lyons Wallcoverings in Sydney, and Clunies-Ross Packman Handprynts, later known as Masterscreen (a subsidiary of Wallpaper Importers Pty Ltd), in Melbourne.

The new Australian manufacturers were clearly riding the crest of a buoyant wallpaper wave. By the late 1960s and early 70s Australians had become among the most prolific users of wallpaper in the world. A fashion for feature walls had passed and in its place returned, for the first time since the 19th century, a desire to cover almost every surface, even the ceiling, with pattern. Innovations such as 'dry-strippable' wallpapers allowed for easy removal and aided frequent redecoration. In 1969 wallpaper specialty shops typically carried around 3000 designs.[34] Australian distributors claimed that the huge increase in the popularity of wallpaper was related to a similar increase in the do-it-yourself market, which included classes in do-it-yourself wallpaper hanging. In 1977 the popular designs of English wallpaper manufacturer Laura Ashley began to be printed under licence by Melbourne's Wallpaper Importers mainly because Australians preferred their papers pre-pasted, which made them easier for the home owner to hang.[35] In the late 70s long-established wallpaper and fabric distributor Wilson Fabrics & Wallpapers (formerly known as A G Wilson) opened its own screen-printing plant under the brand name Signature Handprints. But arguably the most notable new player in the wallpaper industry in terms of size and popularity was Australian Wallcovering Manufacturers. By the late 1970s this company had used the latest rotogravure printing technique to capture as much as 20% of the local market. The Melbourne-based firm, run by husband and wife team Dick and Adrienne Barrington, also produced fabrics and paints to create complete decorative schemes.[36]

The fickle fashion in home decorating was to change again: by 1983 Australians were using just a third of the amount of wallpaper they had used in the mid-70s and were buying less wallpaper than nearly any other country in the Western world.[37] There was a move to plain, undecorated surfaces, which persisted in Australia until the turn of the century. There has since been a gradual return to pattern, though often in commercial spaces and restaurants rather than homes. After virtually disappearing during the 1990s, with the exception of those reproducing historic designs, wallpaper manufacturers have again emerged in Australia. Sydney retailers Chee Soon & Fitzgerald have been at the forefront of the revival, manufacturing a range of new designs which, together with reproduction of Florence Broadhurst's wallpapers by Signature Prints, have helped to inspire market interest.

For more than 200 years wallpaper has offered Australians a colourful and often practical background to domestic life. In the future, fashions will undoubtedly come and go but it is difficult to imagine a return to the halcyon days of the late 19th century when wallpaper was used almost everywhere in the home. New technologies and new designers and manufacturers will have a say in the ongoing relationship between Australians and wallpaper. However, as long as Australians desire colour, pattern and texture rather than plain painted walls, there will be a place for wallpaper in our homes and public buildings.

[1] C Bruce Allen, *Rudimentary treatise on cottage building: or, hints for improving the dwellings of the labouring classes*, 3rd ed, John Weale, London, 1857, p39.

[2] David Adams (ed), *The letters of Rachel Henning*, Penguin, Melbourne, 1969 (reprinted 1979), p143.

[3] Fred Harrison, 'Papers on Australian building and bush work', *Building & Engineering Journal*, Melbourne, 13 July 1889, p46. Quoted in Miles Lewis, *Australian building: a cultural investigation*, 11.02.4, viewed 20 July 2009, <http://www.mileslewis.net/australian-building>

[4] Lara Kriegel, *Grand designs: labour, empire, and the museum in Victorian culture*, Duke University Press, Durham, 2007, pp157–8.

[5] 'How to paper a room', *Town & Country Journal*, Sydney, 23 November 1872, p653. See also Terence Lane & Jessie Serle, *Australians at home: a documentary history of Australian domestic interiors from 1788 to 1914*, Oxford University Press, Melbourne, 1990, pp143–4.

[6] Harrison, op cit, p46.

[7] 'Unsanitary paperhangings', *Australasian Decorator and Painter*, Sydney, 1 January 1908.

[8] 'Poisoned by old wall paper', *Town & Country Journal*, Sydney, 22 March 1902, p19.

[9] Quoted in Lane & Searle, op cit, p144.

[10] 'Arsenic in paperhangings', *British Medical Journal*, London, 9 January 1858, p39.

[11] Adams, op cit, p143.

[12] 'Practical notes on domestic art, no IV', *Brisbane Courier*, 20 March 1878, p6.

[13] 'Art in the home: some hints on furnishing our Australian homes', *Illustrated Sydney News*, 6 March 1890, p8.

[14] *Australasian Decorator and Painter*, Sydney, 1 June 1914, p238; 1 July 1920, p280.

[15]*Decorator & Painter for Australia & New Zealand*, Sydney, 11 June 1938, p446.

[16]*Sydney Morning Herald*, 17 January 1852, p6.

[17]'Art notes: house decoration', *Sydney Mail* [suppl], 5 January 1878, p6.

[18]'Hanging wall paper', *Brisbane Courier*, 22 March 1873, p7; 'Gipsy's notes', *Town & Country Journal*, Sydney, 11 February 1882, p268.

[19]*Artistic homes; or, how to furnish with taste: a handbook for all housekeepers*, Ward, Lock & Co, London, 1880, p21.

[20]*Town & Country Journal*, Sydney, 11 February 1882, p268.

[21]*Annual statement of the trade of the Commonwealth of Australia with the United Kingdom, British possessions and foreign countries for the year 1903*, New South Wales Office of Government Statistician, Sydney, 1904.

[22]Alan Victor Sugden and John Ludlam Edmondson, *A history of English wallpaper: 1509–1914*, Batsford, London, 1925, p196.

[23]*Annual statement of the trade of the United Kingdom with foreign countries and British possessions*, [various years: 1855–1939], House of Commons Parliamentary Papers, London.

[24]*Australasian Decorator and Painter*, 1 September 1907, p288; 1 April 1920, p177.

[25]*The Argus*, 10 April 1851, p1.

[26]*Intercolonial Exhibition of Australasia, Melbourne 1866–67*, p36; *Official record of the Sydney International Exhibition, 1879*, p32.

[27]*Australasian Decorator and Painter*, 1 October 1920, p9; 1 September 1921, p322.

[28]'Interior decoration in Australia', *The Home*, Sydney, June 1928, p27.

[29]William L Richardson (ed), *Ramsay's architectural and engineering catalogue*, Melbourne, 1941, ch27.

[30]*Decorator & Painter for Australia & New Zealand*, Sydney, 15 April 1965, p5.

[31]*Sydney Morning Herald*, 26 February 1960, p13.

[32]*Decorator & Painter for Australia & New Zealand*, Sydney, 15 October 1963, p15.

[33]*Australian Home Beautiful*, Melbourne, March 1959, pp7&20.

[34]*Australian Home Beautiful*, Melbourne, November 1969, p11.

[35]*Australian Home Beautiful*, Melbourne, October 1977, pp71–2.

[36]*Belle*, Sydney, November/December 1979, p133.

[37]'What's happening to wallpapers? Well ...', *Sydney Morning Herald*, 14 April 1983, pp18–20.


**Page 4: Poppies foil wallpaper**, c1973, from an apartment in Bondi Beach, Sydney
**Page 10: Fragment of a Gothic-Revival design**, c1846, used in the first-floor hallway of Rosedale, Campbell Town, Tasmania. Gift of Clive Lucas, Stapleton & Partners
**Page 17: 'Pillar and arch' wallpaper fragment**, c1849, used in the first-floor hallway of Richmond Villa, Sydney
**Page 22:** Arsenic-green fragment, early 1840s, the first of 11 layers of wallpaper uncovered in the parlour of a worker's cottage in Pyrmont, Sydney. Gift of Kim White & Lester Oehm

he repeated more
she kne
Caraven. 'Speak
patient.
disgraceful
his roof—to all
ve me
tion.'
to speak, madam, unless
lieutenant to be
did
s of old turn a haughtier face
One of the ea
ner fee than she turned
to him—proud,
deed who knew
defiant, unbending
Oldys; and Hi
'I would not
to him n
thought,
chance, one da
if
She mi
stood as a
yo
st
Arthur,
id the earl. 'I have been
is quite fair; E
you said, and I do not like it.
You know more,
not like it.'
a wager—you kn
werd.
She never fo
he said. 'I am not always
turned to her..
ma
I—I have a good temper
'Lady Carav
gener
en I am angry I forget myself.
my congratulati
Do not me.'
matters almost a
'I have no wish to irritate you,' she repl
with quiet dignity. 'Say what you have
that I may go quickly.
'I have to say this, Lady Cam
must not speak to me again
—never; I cannot
venswer
ag
to di
ce, as well a
nds can be he
se, knocks
ten people li
ay. Wat
if some
igat

**Wallpaper 'sandwich'**, seven layers plus newspaper lining, 1870s–1920, from a timber slab hut in Berrima, New South Wales. The low cost of wallpaper from the mid-19th to early 20th centuries meant that Australians could regularly redecorate their homes. Installing new wallpaper over old was a quick and common way to achieve a fresh, new look.

**Prussian blue fragment**, c1850, the third oldest of 11 layers of wallpaper found beneath timber panelling in the parlour of a worker's cottage in Pyrmont, Sydney. Gift of Kim White & Lester Oehm. Following the mechanisation of wallpaper production in 1839 even the humblest homes could afford wallpaper from the thousands of new designs available.

**Scroll and flower fragment**, c1860, used in the Hit or Miss Hotel, Hamilton, Tasmania. Gift of Clive Lucas, Stapleton & Partners. Louis-Revival-style furnishings were often used in homes in the mid-19th century. Features such as elaborate scrolls, cartouches and cascading flowers could make even the humblest room look sumptuous.

**Wallpaper sample**, manufactured by Charles J Gordon, London, England, tipped in to the *Journal of Design and Manufactures*, vol 2, no 9, November 1849, London. This sample appears under the heading 'Cheap English paper-hanging' and is described as 'novel and pleasing' and 'suitable to hang prints on in gilt frames, especially for a small room.'

**Abstract design fragment**, 1850s, used in the Hit or Miss Hotel, Hamilton, Tasmania. Gift of Clive Lucas, Stapleton & Partners. This design would be easy to confuse with late-1960s psychedelia. It demonstrates that primary colours were widely used in wallpapers and furnishings of the period.

**Imitation stone fragment**, c1860, used in the Mulwaree Inn (now Garroorigang Historic Home) near Goulburn, New South Wales. Gift of the Hume family. Imitation stone and marble wallpapers were a common choice for hotels in the late 19th century but were also used in private residences, especially to decorate entrance halls and stairwells.

**Imitation painted plasterwork frieze**, 1860s, used in the former reading room of New South Wales Parliament House. Wallpaper friezes that imitated plasterwork were used extensively during the late 19th century. They were typically hung high on the wall at the level of the cornice, and shading was often part of the design for a three-dimensional effect.

**Embossed flock sample** from William Woollams & Co, London, England, c1881. The English *Art Journal* of November 1883 described this type of wallcovering as 'a very ingeniously embossed flock of considerable relief and great richness, simulating, indeed, modelled plasterwork in its surface, and capable of almost infinite variety in its colour treatment'.

**Flock wallpaper**, late 1860s, used in New South Wales Parliament House. Although this floral design is printed, the brown background is flock, manufactured by adhering fragments of 'powdered' wool (often the trimmings from woollen cloth) to paper. Flock was designed to imitate the fabric hangings that had long been used in wealthy homes.

**Nursery pattern**, c1888, used at Terragong, Merriwa, New South Wales. Gift of Clive Lucas, Stapleton & Partners. From the 1870s, specialised nursery wallpapers became increasingly common in middle-class homes, many with illustrations adapted from children's books. This detail shows scenes from the English tale *Dick Whittington and his cat*.

43

**Bird detail** from dado wallpaper, c1891, used along the stair hall of a terrace in Woollahra, Sydney. Gift of Annette & Eric Klein. This detail shows a section of dado and border, part of a decorative scheme that also had a fill and frieze. Dividing up the wall in this way was characteristic of late-19th-century interior decoration.

**Floral wallpaper fragment**, 1890s, the oldest of three layers uncovered in a bedroom at Mulgunnia, Trunkey Creek, New South Wales

**'Buttercup & daisy'** in two colourways, designed by C F A Voysey for Essex & Co, England, 1893. Charles Voysey was a highly influential English architect and designer of the late 19th and early 20th centuries. He believed in simplicity in decoration. This wallpaper demonstrates his preference for using just two or three colours, usually in similar tones.

**'The Aylsham'** in two colourways, designed by C F A Voysey for Essex & Co, England, 1893. Charles Voysey was a prolific designer and his patterns appeared on wallpapers, textiles, carpets and tiles for some of the leading English companies of the late 19th and early 20th centuries.

**Embossed wallpaper**, c1910, used as a dado decoration in the entrance hall of a house in Chatswood, Sydney. Gift of Paul Storm. Embossed wallcoverings with exotic names like Anaglypta, Lignomur and Cordelova enjoyed widespread use in the late 19th and early 20th centuries. They came in a huge variety of designs and were hard-wearing and easy to clean.

**Tulips wallpaper**, c1908, the oldest of 26 layers of wallpaper uncovered in the living room of a timber slab hut in Prospect, west of Sydney. Gift of Clive Lucas, Stapleton & Partners. This extraordinary number of wallpapers, installed over a period of around 50 years, shows that the walls of this hut were re-covered at intervals of less than two years.

**Swan frieze**, c1905, used at Camelot, Narellan, New South Wales. This design has been printed as a mirror image along both edges of this roll. The paperhanger would cut the wallpaper down the middle to produce two lengths of frieze. Landscape and other picturesque scenes on friezes became immensely popular in the first decade of the 20th century.

**Wall panel decoration**, manufactured in England, c1905–10, used at Camelot, Narellan, New South Wales. These two wallpapers were designed as parts of one wall treatment. 'The rose bower' pattern to the left was hung on the upper part of the wall; the design to the right was installed directly below it.

**Rose frieze**, cl905, used at Camelot, Narellan, New South Wales. In the first decade of the 20th century, friezes became ubiquitous as the most important element of wall decoration. They were often hung above a complementary body paper that was comparatively subdued in colour and design.

**Striped fragment**, c1910, used in the pantry at Clifton Grove, Orange, New South Wales. Gift of Clive Lucas, Stapleton & Partners. The use of bright, out-of-register colour was typical of experimentation in early-20th-century wallpaper manufacture. This wallpaper was 'overprinted' two or three times to achieve unusual effects.

**Stripe and Art Nouveau patterns**, c1910, found in an outbuilding in Pitt Town, New South Wales. These two papers would have been inexpensive purchases in their day. On the right is an example of a 'pulp', in which the colour of the paper itself has been used as the background colour. It is now slightly darkened with age.

**Chintz pattern**, manufactured by Arthur Sanderson & Sons Ltd, England, 1911. Chintz wallpaper designs featuring lush foliage, colourful birds and ripe fruit were a fashionable choice in the early 20th century. Originally an Indian fabric design, chintz was introduced to Western countries in the 17th century and has proven to be enduringly popular.

**Poppies pattern**, manufactured by Arthur Sanderson & Sons Ltd, England, 1922, used at Rose Bay Lodge, Rose Bay, Sydney

**Chinoiserie pattern**, manufactured by Wall Paper Manufacturers Ltd, England, 1924. Gift of Bruce MacLeod. In 1922 the *Australasian Decorator and Painter* announced that 'the new season's goods will include something entirely new in design and colouring – the "semi-orient" style – the oriental feeling in design … adapted to English tastes and needs'.

**Geometric floral pattern and matching frieze**

from wallpaper sample book, France, 1920s

**Geometric friezes** from a sample book distributed by Clarkson Ltd, Adelaide, 1939. By the 1930s, wall surfaces in the home had become more textured. Favoured colours included beige and other shades of brown with geometric or 'jazz' friezes in autumnal tones that added key splashes of colour to a room.

**Cut-out wallpaper**, manufactured by Wall Paper Manufacturers Ltd, England, c1927. In the case of a 'cut-out' wallpaper, the central design was supplied perforated on a roll for easy removal. The design would typically have been installed as part of a panel decoration, a device in the 1920s and 30s that allowed a degree of decorative freedom.

**'The Kelso' frieze**, manufactured by Morrison's, Sydney, 1920s. Designed to be applied under the cornice or below the picture rail, this wallpaper comes from a collection of four books of friezes by the same manufacturer. Most designs are represented in a number of colourways and all are hand printed with a combination of woodblocks and stencils.

**Wallpaper sample** from *Album PR Nouveautés*, distributed by P R Paris, France, 1937–38. This stylish and bold wallpaper design would have been an expensive choice in its day. However, it is likely to have been installed on only a section of the wall and used in conjunction with paints and other wallpapers in complementary colours.

**Venetian scene**, Lancastria brand, manufactured by Wall Paper Manufacturers Ltd, England, early 1950s, and provenanced to Robert Lloyd and Tinker Tailor Interiors, Sydney. Gift of Chee Soon & Fitzgerald. Wallpapers depicting exotic places, designed for a feature wall, allowed 1950s home owners to travel vicariously before the age of mass tourism.

**Wrought-iron pattern**, Lancastria brand, manufactured by Wall Paper Manufacturers Ltd, England, 1950s. Gift of Chee Soon & Fitzgerald. These companion wallpapers were designed to be used together in the same room, the floral pattern on a feature wall and the plain wrought-iron pattern on one or more of the other wall surfaces.

**Space-age pattern**, manufactured by Wall Paper Manufacturers Ltd, England, c1956, used in a boy's bedroom in Newtown, Sydney. This playful design is inspired by the fantasy of 1950s sci-fi animation and film. It was made to be hung in a young boy's bedroom or playroom and is part of a long history of using pictorial wallpapers in children's rooms.

**Woven fibres pattern** from wallpaper sample book *New seasons wallpapers*, vol 12, distributed by Grace Bros Pty Ltd, Sydney, 1956

**Classic 1950s pattern** in two colourways, from a wallpaper sample book distributed by James Sandy Pty Ltd, Sydney, c1956, and manufactured by Arthur Sanderson & Sons Ltd, England. This design appeared in the *Australian House and Garden* magazine in November 1956 and was described as a 'whimsical Sanderson wallpaper for dining-room or kitchen'.

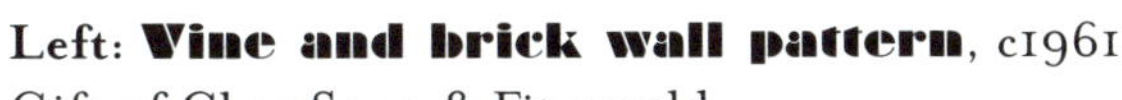

Left: **Vine and brick wall pattern**, c1961.
Gift of Chee Soon & Fitzgerald
Right: **Kitchen shelves pattern** from the sample book
*Laurentian pre-pasted wallpapers & vinyls with selected matching fabrics*,
manufactured by Waldec of Canada Ltd and distributed in
Australia by Comdec Pty Ltd, 1968–69

**Fun fair patterns**, c1957, used in a house in Wahroonga, Sydney. The white colourway was hung in an alcove in the kitchen and the black version decorated the walls and ceiling of a bathroom. These wallpapers formed part of a furnishing scheme by Marion Best Pty Ltd, one of Sydney's most highly regarded interior decorators of the period.

**Cherries pattern**, manufactured by Follot, France, 1960s, from the shop of interior decorators Marion Best Pty Ltd, Sydney. Gift of Chee Soon & Fitzgerald. After an overseas trip in 1949, Marion Best began to import the latest French furnishings. Nobilis and Follot papers were favourites, used with coordinated fabrics in the 1950s and 60s.

**Circus tent pattern**, c1957, used in the games room of a house in Wahroonga, Sydney. This wallpaper formed part of a furnishing scheme by interior decorators Marion Best Pty Ltd. Throughout the 1950s and 60s the tent theme, either as a motif or an actual fabric structure within a room, was a common feature of the company's designs.

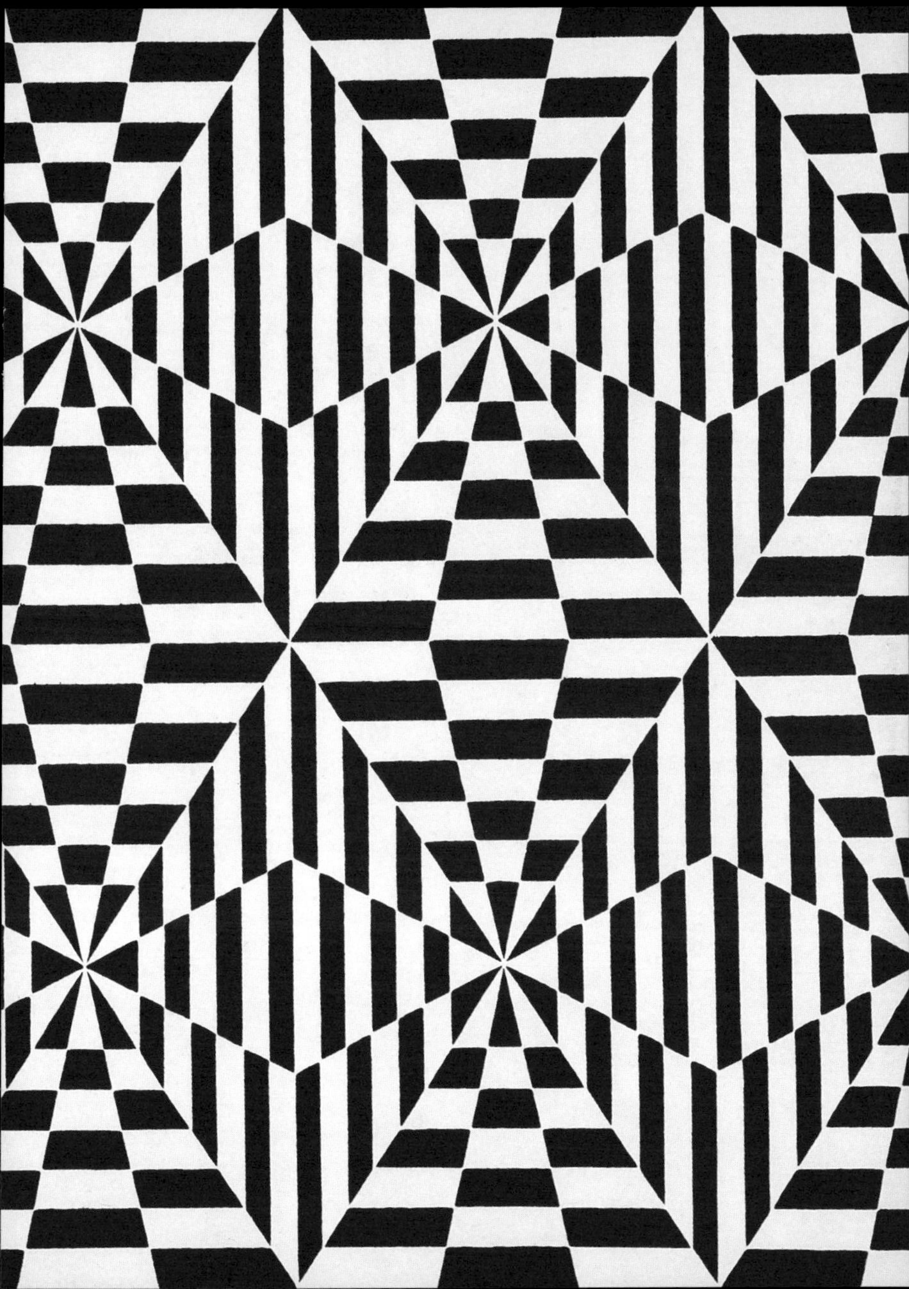

**Stained glass pattern**, Florence Broadhurst Wallpapers Pty Ltd, Sydney, c1968, commissioned by Sydney interior designer Kevin Hambly. Florence Broadhurst and other small Australian manufacturers of the 1970s were favourites of interior decorators as they could produce bespoke wallpapers in small runs and almost any nominated colour combination.

**Psychedelic circles pattern**, manufactured by
United–DeSoto, USA, late 1960s. Gift of Chee Soon &
Fitzgerald. The circle was one of the most recognisable motifs
in pattern design of the 1960s and remained so until well
into the 1970s. Circles were reproduced in a variety of ways —
fragmented, elongated, exploded and in three dimensions.

**'Loch Ness'** in two colourways, manufactured by Inaltera, France, 1970s. Gift of Chee Soon & Fitzgerald

**'Moderne'**, Sunworthy brand, manufactured by Canadian Wallpaper Manufacturers Ltd, Canada, c1969. Gift of Chee Soon & Fitzgerald

110

**Ladybirds pattern**, manufactured by Imperial Wallcoverings, USA, 1970s. Gift of Chee Soon & Fitzgerald

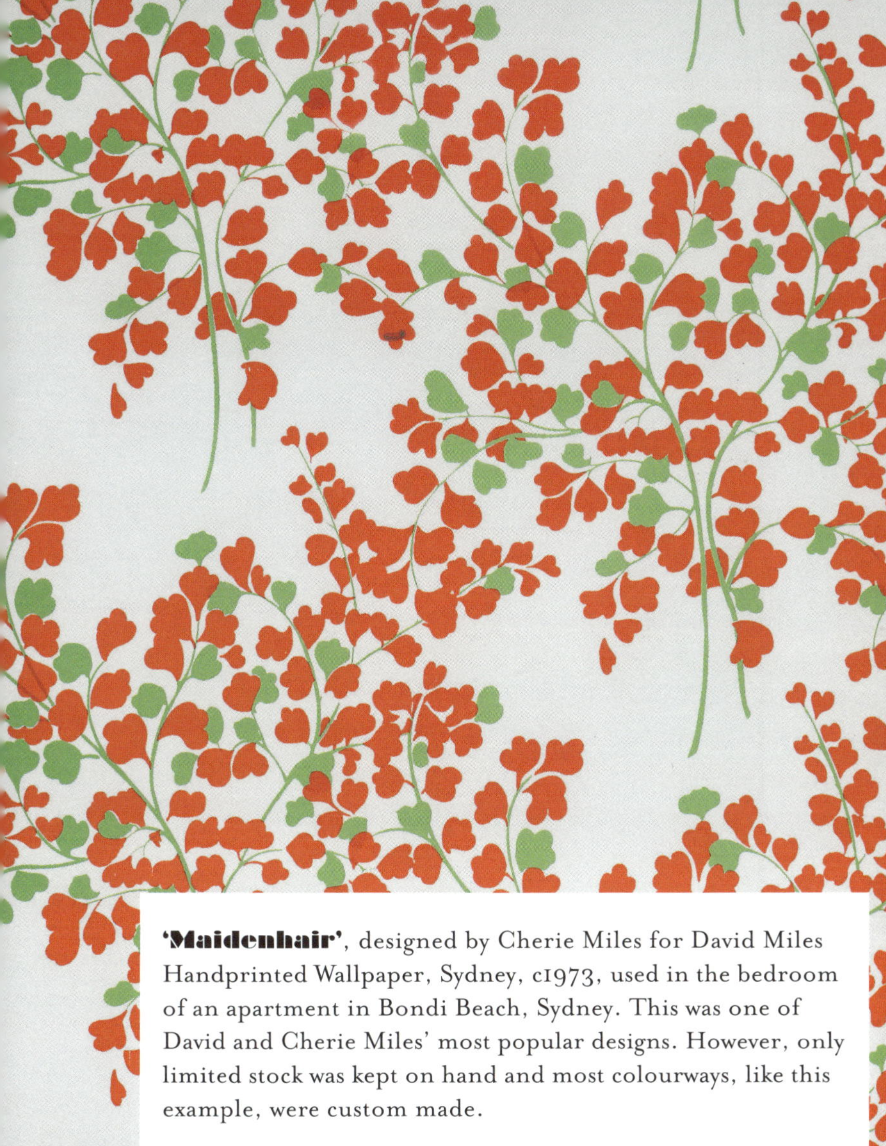

**'Maidenhair'**, designed by Cherie Miles for David Miles Handprinted Wallpaper, Sydney, c1973, used in the bedroom of an apartment in Bondi Beach, Sydney. This was one of David and Cherie Miles' most popular designs. However, only limited stock was kept on hand and most colourways, like this example, were custom made.

**Flower power pattern**, c1972, part of a roll used to paper the kitchen of a house in Mosman, Sydney. Gift of Joy Hughes

**Birds in the clouds pattern** from the wallpaper
sample book *Voyage 85*, Hume Internationale Wallcoverings,
West Germany, 1985

**Blue birds and flowers pattern**, early 1980s, part of a roll left over from papering the bathroom of a house in Mosman, Sydney. Gift of Mrs Helen Perkins

**Toile pattern**, c1993, used to paper the main bedroom of an apartment in Elizabeth Bay, Sydney. Gift of A Chambers. This wallpaper is an imitation of *toile de Jouy*, a type of printed fabric that originated in 18th-century France and typically depicted a pastoral scene printed in a single colour on a white background.

**'Buttons'**, designed by Casey Khik for Chee Soon
& Fitzgerald, Sydney, c2002. Gift of Chee Soon &
Fitzgerald. This design was first produced as a rug, c1999,
for the Australian manufacturer Customweave Pty Ltd.
It was adapted and printed as a wallpaper three years later.

# further reading

Lesley Hoskins (ed), *The papered wall: the history, patterns and techniques of wallpaper*, 2nd ed, Thames and Hudson, London, 2005.

Lesley Jackson, *20th century pattern design: textile & wallpaper pioneers*, Mitchell Beazley, London, 2002.

Terence Lane & Jessie Serle, *Australians at home: a documentary history of Australian domestic interiors from 1788 to 1914*, Oxford University Press, Melbourne, 1990.

Phyllis Murphy, *Historic wallpapers in Australia, 1850–1920*, Castlemaine Art Gallery and Historical Museum, Victoria, 1996.

Gill Saunders, *Wallpaper in interior decoration*, V&A, London, 2002.

Alan Victor Sugden & John Ludlam Edmondson, *A history of English wallpaper: 1509–1914*, Batsford, London, 1925.

Sally Webster (ed), *British wallpapers in Australia 1870–1940*, Historic Houses Trust of New South Wales, Sydney, 1995.

## Historic Houses Trust of New South Wales

All of the wallpaper fragments and rolls featured in this book, and a selection of papers from sample books held in the collection, can be viewed on the HHT website at **www.hht.net.au/research/museum_collections**

Visit the Caroline Simpson Library & Research Collection at The Mint, 10 Macquarie Street, Sydney NSW 2000, or online at **www.hht.net.au/research/library**

For HHT products go to **shop.hht.net.au**

**www.hht.net.au**

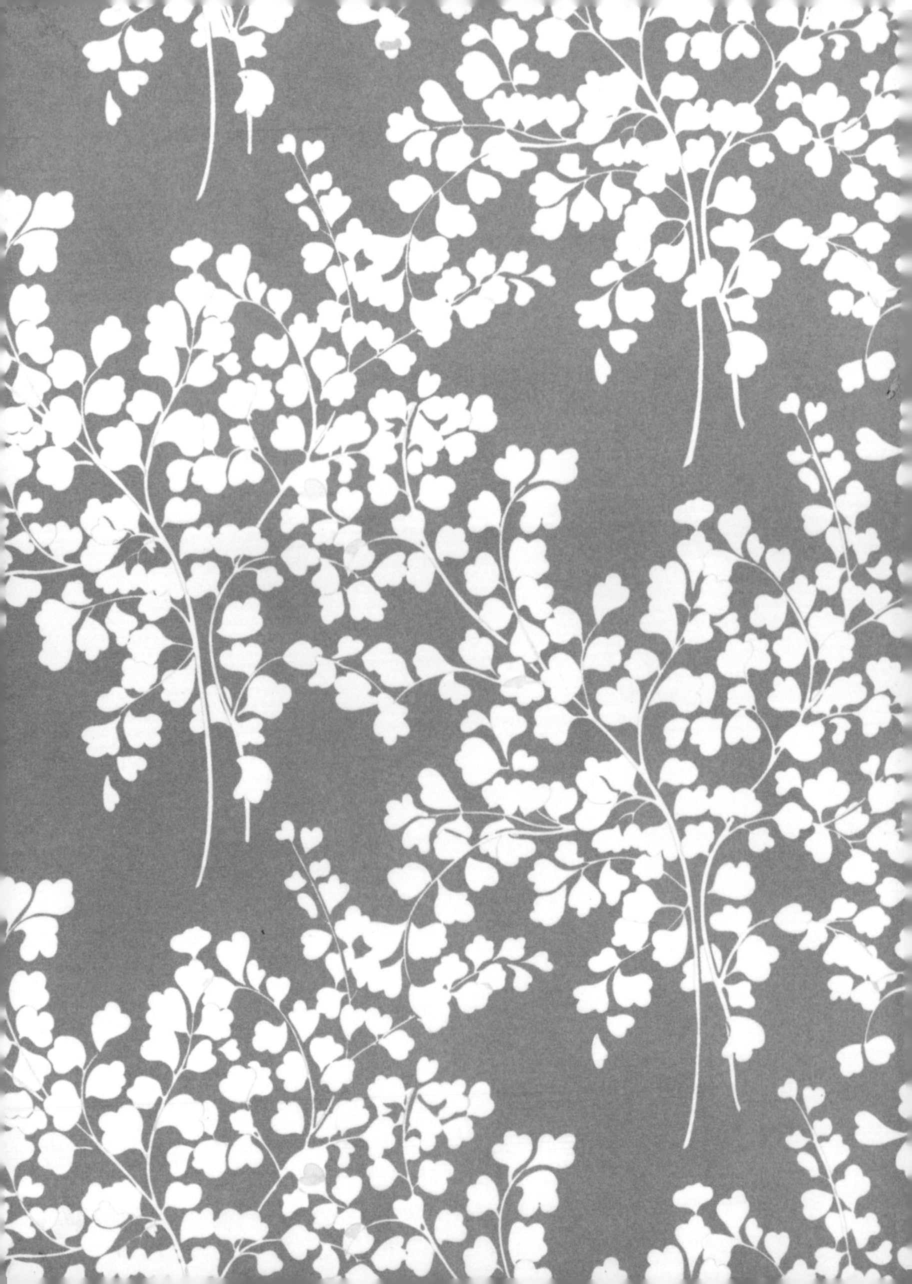